MY VERY FIRST

PRESCHOOL PRESS ®

SEE & KNOW DICTIONARY

Under the supervision of
Dr. Richard E. Wylie

PRESCHOOL PRESS is a trademark of Playmore Inc.,
Publishers and Waldman Publishing Corp.
New York, N.Y.

**Playmore, Inc. Publishers
Under arrangement with Waldman Publishing Corp.
New York, New York**

Food We Eat

FOOD WE EAT

Directions

When working with Food We Eat, do the following:

1. Parent: Read the story or poem with your child. Stop to discuss the key words.

2. Parent: Say each word and point to the corresponding picture. Have your child do the same.

3. Child: Complete the "To do" activity.

4. Child: Color the picture and then show the picture to a friend.

5. Child and Parent: Talk about the pictures and the words. Ask such questions as:
   - What is your favorite food? Why?
   - What types of food don't you like? Why?
   - Where does the food come from?

A a

animal crackers

appetite

Hungry? Oh yes. I have an <u>appetite</u> big enough to eat an elephant. . . an elephant <u>animal cracker</u> that is.

To do:

Circle the elephant.

A **a**

apples

apple pie

<u>Apples</u> grow on apple trees.
They are juicy and sweet to eat
just as they are.
They can also be made into <u>apple</u> <u>pie</u>!

To do: Color the red.

B b

 baker

 bread

Sniff the air
and you can tell
that the <u>baker</u> is busy
baking <u>bread</u>.

To do:

Draw a loaf of bread. ➡

B b

butter

banana

For a snack you can have
some bread and <u>butter</u>.
Or would you rather
have a <u>banana</u>?

To
do:

Draw what you like to eat.

B b

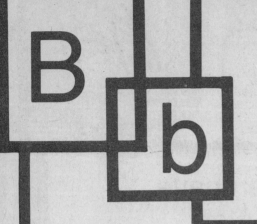

barbecue

beef

The coals are hot,
the flames are jumping.
The <u>beef</u> is cooking.
It's a <u>barbecue</u>.

To do: Color the picture.

C c

cake

candy

Pretend that it's your birthday
And this <u>cake</u> is for you.
You may even get
Some <u>candy</u> too!

To do:

Color the 🎂 red.
Color the 🍬 green, blue and yellow.

C c

cereal

chicken

<u>Cereal</u> is good at breakfast,
and you may have <u>chicken</u>
for lunch or dinner.
Which one would you like to eat
right now?

To do:

Draw the cereal you like best ▶

C c

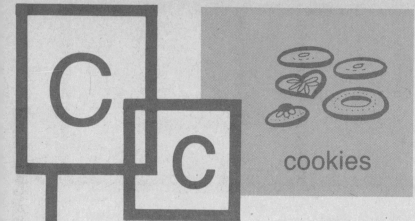

cookies

cooking

Mom's in the kitchen
and I know that she is <u>cooking</u>.
I hope she is making
chocolate <u>cookies</u>!

To do:

Color the  in the picture
to make them chocolate.

C c

crackers

crumbs

My little brother loves
to eat <u>crackers</u>.
But he leaves <u>crumbs</u> behind him
wherever he goes.

To
do:

What would you use
to clean up crumbs?

dessert

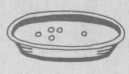
diet

If you want to lose weight
you'll have to <u>diet</u>.
So don't eat such a
big <u>dessert</u>!

To do: Color the a bright color.

D d

doughnut

drink

What is round with a hole in the middle?
It's a <u>dough</u>nut!
What would you like to <u>drink</u>
With your <u>dough</u>nut?

To do:

How many are in a dozen? _____

write the number

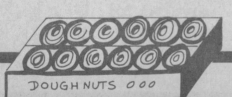

E e

eat

eggs

Scrambled or fried or poached,
softboiled or hardboiled.
Eggs are fun because there are
so many ways you can eat them.

To do:

Where do come from?

F f

food

fork

When I eat an apple or a cookie,
I hold it in my hand.
But some <u>food</u> I eat with a <u>fork</u>.

To do:

Draw a picture of a kind of food you would eat with a .

F f

farm

Most of the food we eat
is grown on a <u>farm</u>.
Can you name the foods
found on this farm?

To do: Circle everything in the picture
that you might eat.

F f

fish

flour

There's <u>flour</u> in many foods we eat,
in cakes and cookies and bread.
I like to eat bread with fried <u>fish</u>

To do:

Draw a picture of a fish.

F f

fruit

Different <u>fruits</u> are different colors,
Red, orange, yellow, blue and green.
It's fun to have fresh <u>fruit</u> to eat
For meals or in between.

FRUIT ☆

To do: Look at the picture and color
the fruits that you like to eat.

G g

gingerbread

graham crackers

When it's time for a snack,
Try some <u>gin</u>gerbread.
Or maybe you'd like
<u>Graham</u> <u>crackers</u> instead.

To do:

Which snack do you like best?

H h

harvest

The food on the farm is ripe and grown.
And now it's <u>harvest</u> time.
All the food is picked and taken away
to be sold in markets and stores.

To do:

Circle the food that grows in a field. ▶

H h

ham

hamburger

What will I eat for lunch today?
Should it be a <u>ham</u> sandwich?
Or a juicy <u>hamburger</u>
with lots of ketchup?

To do: Color the hamburger brown.

H h

honey

hot dog

For a snack, put some <u>honey</u>
on your toast.
For lunch you can put mustard
or relish or ketchup on your <u>hot dog</u>.

To do:

What would you not
put on a hot dog?

MUSTARD

ice

ice cream

Let's make <u>ice</u> <u>cream</u> the way Grandma did. Put lots of <u>ice</u> and cream in the machine and turn the handle for a long, long time.

To do:

Color the your favorite flavor.

jam

jelly

You may have some jelly.
Or you may have some jam.
They both taste great
on toast or muffins or bread.

To do: Write the letter J j. _____

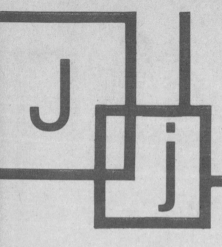

J j

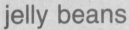

jelly beans

juice

Jelly beans and juice
Make a delicious snack.
Eat them now before you go out
or later, when you come back.

To do:

Color the jelly beans red, green,
blue and orange.

K k

knife

ketchup

<u>Ketchup</u> makes many things
taste even better.
Pour some on your hamburger
and spread it with your <u>knife</u>.

To do: Add the letter K
to make a word.

___nife

L l

lemons

lemonade

<u>Lemons</u> are very sour to eat.
But a glass of <u>lemonade</u>
is an ice-cold treat.

Color the and the yellow.

L l

lollipops

licorice

<u>Licorice</u> and <u>lollipops</u>
are really good to eat.
Please come share some with me.
They both are very sweet.

To do:

Color the in your favorite flavors.

L l

lunch   lettuce

What time is it?
It's 12 o'clock and time for <u>lunch</u>.
Please put a little <u>lettuce</u> on
my sandwich.

To
do:

Make the clock say 12 o'clock.

Mm

meat

Roastbeef, bacon, steak and lamb.
Hamburgers, hotdogs and ham.
They're many different kinds of <u>meat</u>.
What is your favorite one to eat?

To do:

Color your favorite meat
in the picture.

M m

maple syrup

market

<u>Maple</u> <u>syrup</u> comes from a tree
but Mom buys it at the <u>market</u>.
And I put it on my pancakes
with lots of butter!

To do:

_____

Write the word maple. _____

_____

M m

milk

milk shake

<u>Milk</u> is a delicious drink.
It's also good for you.
Sometime for a special treat
Try a <u>milk</u> <u>shake</u>, too!

To do:

Count the glasses of milk.

Write the number. _____

N n Nutrition

Do you eat?

fish

eggs

meat

bread

fruit

chicken

vegetables

milk

If you do, you are
getting good nutrition!
And that means you will
grow strong and healthy.

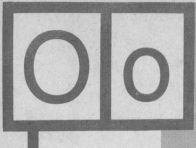

overeat

omelet

My dad's a great cook.
When he makes an <u>omelet</u>,
it's so good that I have to
be careful not to <u>overeat</u>!

To do: Use the colors blue, green, yellow
and brown to color the picture.

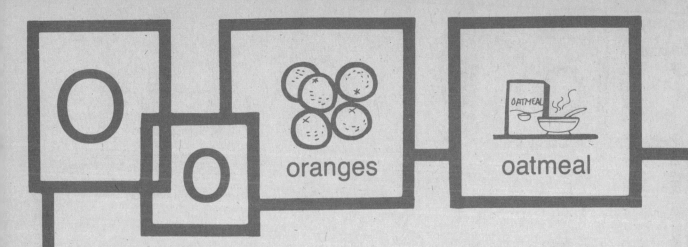

oranges

oatmeal

Oatmeal is good to eat
for breakfast.
Oranges are good for breakfast
and for a snack at almost any time.

To do: Count the oranges on the plate.

Write the number. _____

P p

pancakes

peanut butter

<u>Pancakes</u> for breakfast.
<u>Peanut butter</u> for lunch.
That's the way I like to eat!

To do:

Draw what you would like for dinner. ➡

P p

pie

plate

The <u>pl</u>ate is empty.
The <u>pie</u> is gone.
Who do you think ate the pie?

To do:

Write the first letter of
the words pie and plate.

P p

popcorn

potatoes

<u>Potatoes</u> can be baked or mashed or even fried or boiled.
But <u>popcorn</u> always pops!

To do:

Draw a bag of popcorn.

Q q

quart

Just think, a whole quart of ice cream just for me!

To do:

Circle the quart.

R r

roastbeef

rice

Last night we had a very good dinner!
We had <u>roastbeef</u> and vegetables
and <u>rice</u>.

To do: Color the picture.

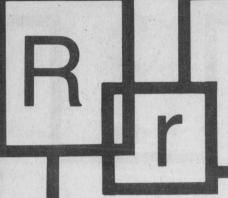

restaurant

rolls

Tonight we are going to eat in a <u>restaurant</u>.
I'm going to eat lots of <u>rolls</u> with butter.

To do:

Count the Write the number. _____

S s

salad

sandwiches

Let's go on a picnic!
We'll have <u>salad</u> and <u>sandwiches</u>
And I hope we don't have too many ants!

To do: Place an X on things you might use in a .

S s

seafood

supermarket

<u>Seafood</u> is fish
that fishermen catch in the sea.
But you can buy some
at the <u>supermarket</u>.

To do:

Circle the seafood.

S S

snack

soda

Hey, Tom, let's stop
And have a <u>snack</u>!
I have some <u>soda</u>
In my pack.

To do:

Draw your favorite snack.

S s

soup

spoon

I like a bowl of <u>soup</u> for lunch
On a winter day at noon.
It makes me feel all warm inside,
And I eat it with a <u>spoon</u>.

To do:

Draw a picture of a spoon.

toast

tea

Have some <u>tea</u> and <u>toast</u>.
What do you like best on your <u>toast</u>?
Butter or jam or honey?

To do:

Color the toast brown.

Color the jam red.

T t

Thanksgiving

turkey

On <u>Thanksgiving</u> our family always eats <u>turkey</u>. What does your family eat?

To do: Complete the drawing to make a turkey.

U u

upside-down cake

utensils

If you have baking <u>utensils</u>,
you can bake an <u>upside-down</u> <u>cake</u>.
Please bake one, just for me!

To
do:

Color the

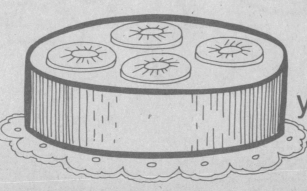

yellow.

vegetables

vitamins

I eat <u>vegetables</u> every day.
There are many different kinds
and they all have <u>vitamins</u>
to keep me strong and healthy.

To do: Color your favorite vegetable.

W W

waffles

watermelon

The letter W begins two
of my favorite foods.
<u>Waffles</u> for breakfast
and <u>watermelon</u> for dessert.

To do:

Write the word waffles._____

X x

There are no foods that begin with the letter X. But you can use the letter X to mark your favorite foods. Put an X in the box next to each food that you really like to eat.

fish ☐

chicken ☐

hamburger ☐

soup ☐

cake ☐

ice cream ☐

apples ☐

pancakes ☐

milk ☐

banana ☐

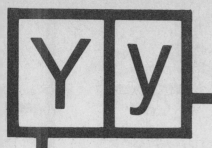 
yam

yogurt

A <u>yam</u> is a kind of potato
that grows underground.
<u>Yogurt</u> is a tasty treat,
especially mixed with fruit.

To do: Which food does not begin
with the letter Y?

Z z

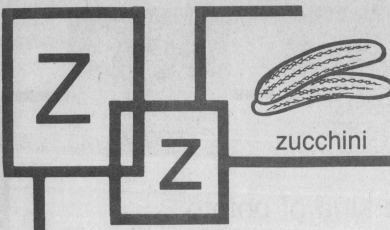

zucchini

zwieback

<u>Zucchini</u> is a vegetable
that I love to eat.
But the baby likes to chew
on a kind of toast called <u>zwieback</u>

To do: Write the letter Z z. _____

Food We Eat Word List

animal crackers
appetite
apple pie
apples

baker
banana
barbecue
beef
bread
butter

cake
candy
cereal
chicken
cookies
cooking
crackers
crumbs

dessert
diet
doughnut
drink

eat
eggs

farm
fish
food
fork
flour
fruit

gingerbread
graham crackers

ham
hamburger
harvest
honey
hot dog

ice
ice cream

jam
jelly
jelly beans
juice

knife
ketchup

lemon
lemonade
lettuce
licorice
lollipops
lunch

maple syrup
market
meat
milk
milk shake

nutrition

oatmeal
omelet
oranges
overeat

pancakes
peanut butter
pie
plate
popcorn
potatoes

quart

restaurant
rice
roastbeef
rolls

salad
sandwiches
seafood
snack
soda

soup
spoon
supermarket

toast
tea
Thanksgiving
turkey

upside-down cake
utensils

vegetables
vitamins

waffles
watermelon

yam
yogurt

zucchini
zwieback

Animals at the Zoo

A VISIT TO THE ZOO

Directions

When working with A Visit to the Zoo, do the following:

1. Parent: Read the short story or poem with your child. Stop to discuss the key words.

2. Parent: Say each word and point to the corresponding picture. Have your child do the same.

3. Child: Complete the "To do" activity.

4. Child: Color the picture and then show the picture to a friend.

5. Child and parent: Talk about the pictures and the words. Ask questions such as:

   - In what type of environment (explain the term) do you think this animal lives?
   - What type of food do you think this animal eats?

A a

alligator

anteater

The <u>alligator</u> likes to sleep
Where the water isn't deep.

Mr. <u>Anteater</u> nibbles all day
On tiny black ants that come his way.

To do: Make the sound of a sleeping  .

antelope

ape

Have you ever seen:

An <u>antelope</u> jumping rope?
Or an <u>ape</u> wearing yellow pants
and cape?

To do: Color the blue

and the yellow.

B b

badger

balloon

While boys and girls with big <u>balloons</u>
Are walking all around

The <u>badger</u> is digging
A hole in the ground.

To do: Which of these would a  use
to dig his hole?

B b

bars

birds

The <u>bars</u> on the cages
Keep the zoo safe for you.

Some cages have glass.
That keeps the <u>birds</u> in, too.

To do: Finish the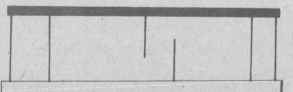

B **b** beaver buffalo

Mr. <u>Beaver</u> chews on a log.
He works very hard all day.

Mr. <u>Buffalo</u> is lazy.
He just walks away.

To do: Color the  brown.

C c

camel

chameleon

Camels come in two styles——
One hump or two.

Chameleons come in different colors.
They can change their colors, too!

To
do: The  changes
color to match his surroundings.
Color the three different colors.

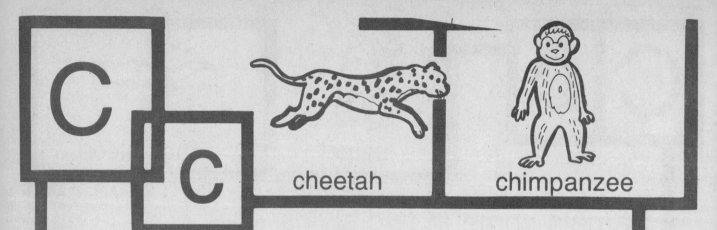

C c

cheetah

chimpanzee

The <u>cheetah</u> runs so fast
She finds it hard to stop.
The <u>chimpanzee</u>, she hangs on tight
So that she will not drop.

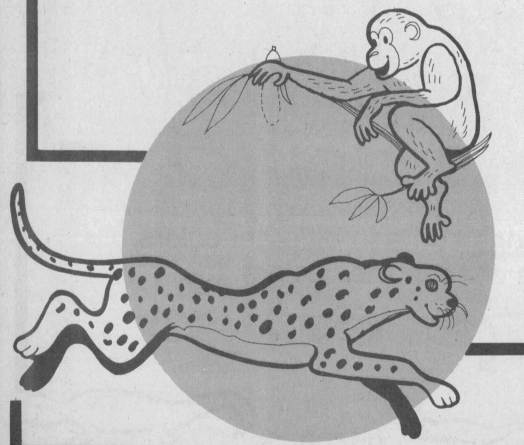

To do: Connect the dots and find out what the chimpanzee is holding in her paw.

C c

coyote

crane

This <u>coyote</u> howls, they say.
All night but never in the day.
Right nearby there stands a <u>crane</u>
With legs so long it needs a cane.

To do:

Write the word crane. _____

D d

deer

donkey

This <u>donkey</u> likes to wear a hat.
It has a big red flower.
The <u>deer</u> just likes to nibble
Hour after hour.

To do: Color the flower in the donkey's hat.

D d

dove

duck

The <u>doves</u> are sitting on their perch,
And you can hear them cooing.
The <u>ducks</u> are always at the pond.
Can you tell what they're doing?

To do: Count the on the pond.

Write the number. _____

E e eagle elephant

The <u>eagle</u>'s wings can carry him
High up in the sky.
Wouldn't it be funny
If <u>ele</u>phants could fly?

To do: Draw a

F f

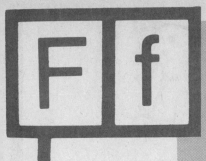

fox

frog

Mrs. <u>Frog</u> lives in the pond.
She sits in the sun on the rocks.
But stalking through the bushes,
Here comes Mrs. <u>Fox</u>.

To do: Draw a rock for
the to sit on.

G g

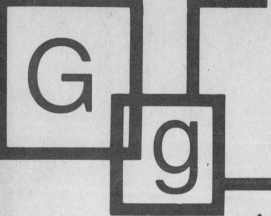

giraffe

gopher

The <u>giraffe</u> is so tall
That his head's in the
trees.

The <u>gopher</u> can be found
Underground, if you please.

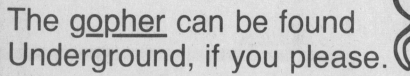

To do: Draw a circle around the tallest
animal on the page.

G g

gorilla

Gorillas are strong.

Gorillas are fierce.

And gorillas can be funny.

To do: Draw a hat on the funny .

H h

happy faces

What do animals think
When we look, smile and laugh
At them?

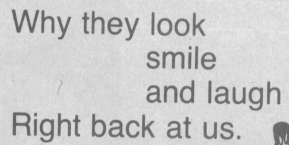

Why they look
smile
and laugh
Right back at us.

To do: Draw a smiling face. ▶

H h

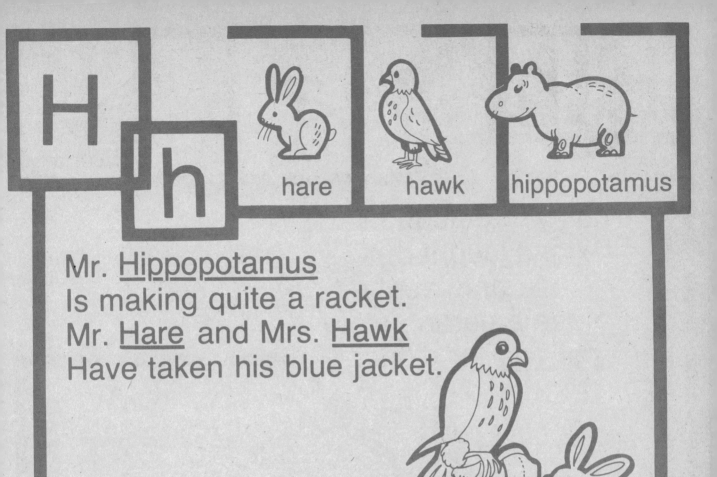

hare

hawk

hippopotamus

Mr. <u>Hippopotamus</u>
Is making quite a racket.
Mr. <u>Hare</u> and Mrs. <u>Hawk</u>
Have taken his blue jacket.

To do: Color a jacket on Mr.

H h

hot dog

hyena

The <u>hyena</u> laughed
  and laughed
    and laughed
To see a heron eating
A <u>hot dog</u> for dinner.

To
do:

Circle what you like
on a .

I i

iguana

He looks like a little dragon
But <u>iguana</u> is his name.
And you don't have to be frightened
For he's really very tame.

To do: Color the  green.

J j

jaguar

The <u>jaguar</u> is a cat
Of notorious speed.
He runs with the swiftness
Of the wind and me.

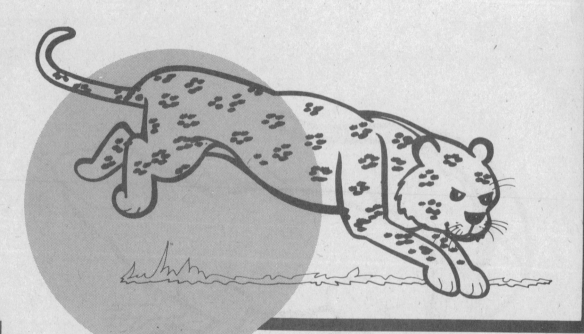

To
do:

Draw something
that is very fast.

K k

kangaroo

This is a mother <u>kangaroo</u>.
She's jumping far and wide.
She carries her baby in a pouch
So he can have a ride.

To do: Color the brown and the grass green.

K k

koala bear

keeper

Soft and gray and fuzzy
Is this little <u>koala bear</u>.
Watch how the <u>keeper</u> of the zoo
Handles him with care.

To do:

Koala bears like to sit in trees.
Draw a tree for this <u>koala bear</u> to sit in.

lamb

leopard

Lambs are soft and gentle.
They make very good pets, too.
But the leopard is ferocious.
He's kept in a cage at the zoo.

To do:

Make the leopard look happy.

lion

llama

The <u>llama</u> is an animal
Who always looks timid and shy.
But the <u>lion</u> always looks so fierce
That they call him the king of beasts.

To do:

Make the  look funny.

monkey

mule

If a <u>monkey</u> and a <u>mule</u>
Lived in cages side by side.
The <u>monkey</u> might jump on the back
of the <u>mule</u>
And take a long, long ride.

To do: Draw a  on the 's head.

N n

nickel   nightingale

My mom gave me a <u>nickel</u>
To spend at the zoo.
I gave it to the <u>nightingale</u>.
He said, "I'll sing for you."

To do: Color the  bright colors.

opossum

ostrich

The <u>ostrich</u> sometimes digs a hole
And buries his head in the ground.

And this <u>opossum</u> in the tree
Is hanging upside down.

Which animal hangs upside down?

O o

otter

owl

This animal likes a sliding board.
His name is Mr. <u>Otter</u>.
The wise old <u>owl</u> is watching
As he slides into the water.

To do: Draw some water for Mr. Otter.

P p

panda

panther

The <u>panda</u> looks like a black and white bear.
He holds his food in his paws.
The <u>panther</u> is really a kind of cat.
Watch out for his very sharp claws!

To do: Color the  black and white.

 parrot

 polar bear

The <u>parrot</u> likes to chatter.
His feathers are very bright.
The <u>polar bear</u> likes the ice and snow.
His fur is always white.

To
do: Color the 🦜 three different colors.

P p

peacock

pelican

The <u>peacock</u> shows his feathers
Of green and blue and white.
While the <u>pelican</u> is thinking
Of the fish she'll eat tonight.

To do: Color the  green, blue and white.

P p

pond

popcorn

peanuts

Sandwiches, <u>peanuts</u> and <u>popcorn</u>
Are things we like to munch.
When we sit by the <u>pond</u> at the zoo
And have a picnic lunch.

To do: Draw a 🦆 on the pond.

Q q

quail

quill

The <u>qu</u>ail was taking her daily walk
When she found a sharp-pointed <u>qu</u>ill.
She knew it belonged to the porcupine
Who lived just up the hill.

To do: Draw a quill. ▶

R r

rabbit

racoon

Richard the <u>rabbit</u>
Eats juicy carrots.

While Rodney, the <u>racoon</u>,
Naps at noon.

To
do: Color the  orange.

R r

rhinoceros

reindeer

The <u>rhinoceros</u> just lumbers around.
He's big and heavy and slow.
But everyone knows that the <u>reindeer</u>
Runs swiftly over the snow.

To do:

Which animal can run faster?

sea lion

seal

The <u>sea lion</u> likes to sit in the sun
And sleep upon a rock.
The <u>seal</u> jumps up and thinks it's fun
To climb on top of a block.

To do: Draw a big in the sky.

tiger

tortoise

Do you know why
The <u>tortoise</u>
Never leaves his house
And the <u>tiger</u>
Never takes off his coat?

To
do:

Tell me why.

U u

umbrella

uniform

The zoo keeper wears a <u>uniform</u>.
His jacket and pants are gray.
He carries a black <u>umbrella</u>
If it's a rainy day.

To do: Draw rain  in the sky.

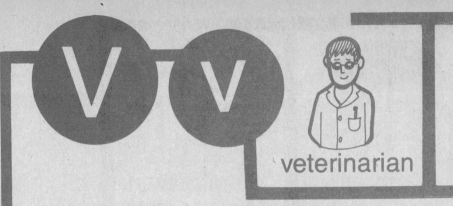

V v

veterinarian

vulture

If an animal is sick
Call the <u>veterinarian</u> , quick!
He's the doctor who knows what to do
For bears and tigers and <u>vultures</u>, too.

To
do: _____

Write the letter Vv. ----------------------------------

_____

W w

wallaby

wart hog

The animal sitting on a couch
Is a <u>wallaby</u> with tail and pouch.

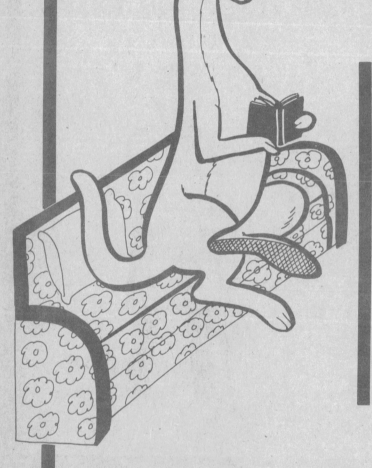

This is a <u>wart hog</u>
Sitting on a log.

To do:

What other animal has a tail and a pouch?

W w

walrus

whale

If you want to weigh a <u>walrus</u>
Just put him on the scale.
Which do you think weighs the most?
The <u>walrus</u> or the <u>whale</u>?

To do:

Color the  gray.

X-ray

The monkey hurt his paw one day.
I think he tripped and fell.
He had to have an <u>X-ray</u>.
But now his paw is well.

To do: Color the monkey brown.

Y y

yellow-billed cuckoo

yak

There goes the <u>y</u>ellow-billed <u>c</u>uckoo,
His suitcase on his back.
He's flying off to visit a friend
Whose name is Yancy <u>Y</u>ak.

To do: Draw a hat on Yancy Yak.

Z z

zebra

zoo

Here's the <u>zebra</u> at the <u>zoo</u>.
He prances left and right.
He looks a little like a horse
With stripes of black and white.

To do: Color the black and white.

Zoo Words

alligator
anteater
antelope
ape

badger
balloon
bars
beaver
birds
buffalo

camel
chameleon
cheetah
chimpanzee
coyote
crane

deer
donkey
dove
duck

eagle
elephant

fox
frog

giraffe
gopher
gorilla

hare
hawk
hippopotamus
hot dog
hyena

iguana

jaguar

kangaroo
keeper
koala bear

lamb
leopard
lion
llama

monkey
mule

nickel
nightingale

opossum
ostrich
otter
owl

panda
panther
parrot

peacock
pelican
picnic
polar bear
pond
popcorn

quail
quill

rabbit
racoon
reindeer
rhinoceros

sea lion
seal

tiger
tortoise

umbrella
uniform

veterinarian
vulture

wallaby
walrus
wart hog
whale

X-ray

yellow-billed
cuckoo

zebra
zoo

Clothes We Wear

CLOTHES WE WEAR

Directions

When working with Clothes We Wear, do the following:

1. Parent: Read the short story with your child. Stop to discuss the story and the picture.

2. Parent: Say each word and point to the key picture. Ask your child to do the same.

3. Child: Complete the "To do" activity.

4. Child: Color the picture and show it to a friend.

5. Child and Parent: Talk about the pictures and the words. Ask such questions as:

- **Why is the person dressed this way?**

- **Where do you think he lives?**
  Where is she going?

- **Have you seen clothes like these? Where?**

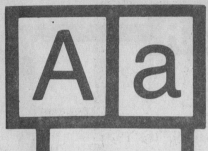  apron

 ascot

Mother wears an <u>apron</u> when she cooks in the kitchen. And Dad wears an <u>ascot</u> when he barbecues.

To do: Color the  yellow.

Color the blue.

B b

belt

Bermuda shorts

Brad needs help getting dressed! He can't wear that plaid <u>belt</u> with those <u>Bermuda shorts</u>.

To do: Draw a [belt] that would look better with Brad's [shorts].

B b

bib

blouse

My baby sister is just learning to eat, so she wears a <u>bib</u> over her <u>blouse</u>.

To do:

Color the  red.

Color the  green.

B b

bonnet

bootees

Babies need very special clothing. Make sure baby has on her <u>bonnet</u> and <u>bootees</u> when you take her for a walk.

To do:

Draw a bonnet. ▶

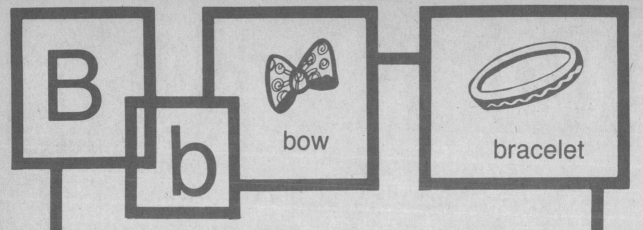

B **b**

bow

bracelet

Becky likes to play dress-up. She wears a pretty <u>bow</u> in her hair and has mother's shiny <u>bracelet</u>.

To do:

Color Becky's and the same color.

C c

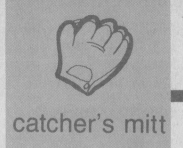

cap

catcher's mitt

Batter up! Casey straightens his <u>cap</u> and checks his <u>catcher's mitt</u>. The big game is ready to begin.

To do: Draw home plate for Casey to stand on.

C c

cleats

coat

The umpire wears a black cap, a black <u>coat</u> and black pants. He wears shoes with <u>cleats</u>.

To do: Color the umpire's uniform black.

C c

cowboy hat

crown

Make-believe is fun. Wear a <u>cowboy hat</u> and pretend you're a rough and tough cowboy. Wear a <u>crown</u> and pretend you're a handsome prince.

To do:

Draw another 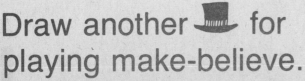 for playing make-believe.

C c

cuffs

cummerbund

David is dressed for the dance. His shirt has ruffles on the <u>cuffs</u> and he has a <u>cummerbund</u> around his waist.

To do:

Draw flowers for David to give to his girlfriend. ▶

D d

diaper

dress

Sometimes Daddy likes to help take care of baby. He changes the <u>diaper</u> and picks out a <u>dress</u> for baby to wear.

To do: Color the green.

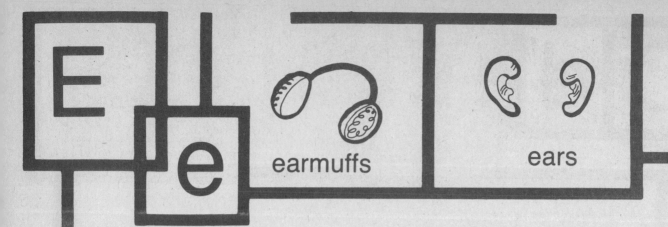

E e

earmuffs

ears

"It's cold and the snow is everywhere! Better put my <u>earmuffs</u> on if I want to keep my <u>ears</u> warm!" said the snowman.

To do:

Draw a scarf to match the snowman's ▶ .

F f

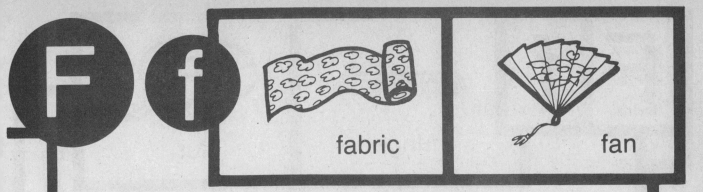

fabric

fan

The Japanese use beautiful silk <u>fabric</u> to make <u>fans</u> for lovely ladies.

To do:

Make pretty designs on the

F f

fringe

fur

When the seamstress makes a dress she might use <u>fur</u> or <u>fringe</u> for trim.

To do:

Put 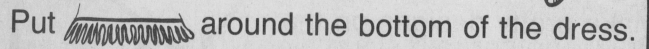 around the bottom of the dress.

G g

galoshes

gloves

<u>Galoshes</u> and <u>gloves</u> are very handy to have if you like sloshing in puddles on wet and rainy days.

To do:

Draw another rain cloud high in the sky.

G g

gowns

grass skirt

If you visit Hawaii you will see ladies in bright flowered <u>gowns</u> and beautiful hula dancers in rustling <u>grass skirts</u>.

To do: Color bright flowers on the gown.

hard hat

helmet

A <u>hard hat</u> is a kind of <u>helmet</u> that a construction worker wears to protect his head.
A football player wears another kind of <u>helmet</u>.

To do:

Color the bright orange.

ice skates

ice-skating skirt

Rebecca is ready for the skating party. See, she has her <u>ice skates</u> and an <u>ice-skating skirt</u>.

To do: Color the ice-skating skirt yellow.

J j

jacket

jeans

The sun is shining. It's a perfect day for hiking. Grab your <u>jacket</u> and your <u>jeans</u> and we'll be on our way!

To do: Draw some patches on the .

J j

jersey

jodhpurs

When you're getting ready to play football, wear your numbered <u>jersey</u>. But if you're going to ride a horse, <u>jodhpurs</u> are what you'll wear.

To do: Finish the number on the .

K k

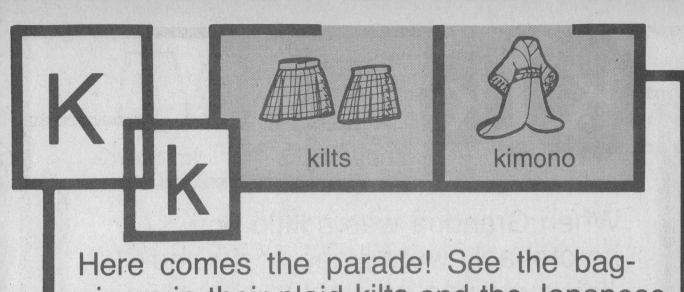

kilts

kimono

Here comes the parade! See the bag-pipers in their plaid <u>kilts</u> and the Japanese dancers in their beautiful silk <u>kimonos</u>.

To do:

Color the red and black.

K k

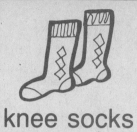
knee socks

knickers

When Grandpa was a little boy he probably wore <u>knee socks</u> and <u>knickers</u> when he went to school.

To do: Color the  brown.

L l

lace

leotards

It's almost time for the play to begin! The actors and actresses, dressed in <u>lace</u> and <u>leotards</u>, are ready for opening night.

To do:

Use your favorite colors for this page.

M m

mittens

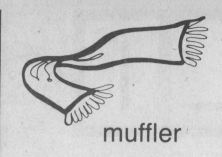

muffler

Gina is going to build a snowman.
She puts on her new red <u>mittens</u>
and wraps her <u>muffler</u> around her
neck.

To do:

Color Gina's muffler to match her mittens.

N n   necklace   necktie

You wear some things on your feet.
You wear some things on your hands.
You wear a <u>necklace</u> or a <u>necktie</u>
around your neck!

To do: Draw stripes on the necktie.

N n

nightgown   nightshirt

Back in the days of covered wagons and log cabins, mama wore a long ruffled <u>nightgown</u> and papa wore a long, flannel <u>nightshirt</u>

To do:

Draw a fire in the fireplace to keep mama and papa warm.

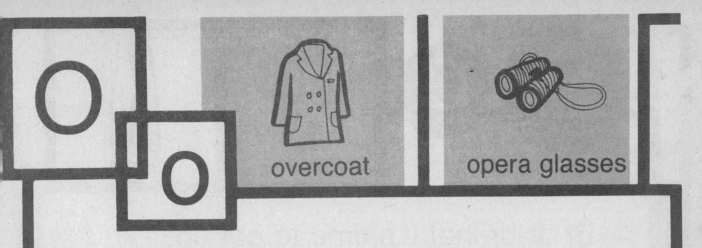

O o

overcoat

opera glasses

Old Mr. Oglethorpe was going to the opera, so he put on his <u>overcoat</u> and put <u>opera glasses</u> in his pocket.

To do:

Draw a hat on Mr. Oglethorpe.

P p

pajamas

pants

Br-br-br-ing! It's time to get up!
Dad will jump out of bed, take off
his <u>pajamas</u>, and get dressed for
work in his shirt and <u>pants</u>.

To do:

Make the alarm clock say 7 o'clock.

P p

petticoat

pinafore

Lisa is 6 years old today! She's getting ready for her birthday party. She's going to wear her brand new <u>petticoat</u> and a pretty flowered <u>pinafore</u>.

To do:

Color the flowers blue on the pinafore.

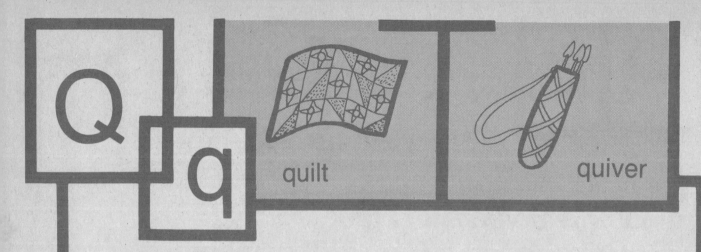

Q q

quilt

quiver

When Sarah and Keith went to
the County Fair, they saw ladies
making a beautiful <u>qu</u>ilt and
a man dressed as an Indian. The
Indian wore a <u>qu</u>iver on his back.

To do: Draw arrows in the .

R r

ribbons

rings

Aunt Betty has many beautiful things.
She wears <u>ribbons</u> in her hair
and shiny <u>rings</u> on all her fingers.

To do:

Make the ribbons many different colors.

R r

robe

rubbers

A <u>robe</u> keeps you nice and warm after your bath.

<u>Rubbers</u> keep your feet nice and dry when you are walking in the rain.

To do: Color the  black.

Color the red.

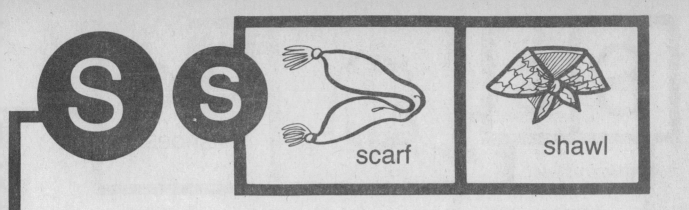

S s scarf shawl

When it's cold and blustery you wear a <u>scarf</u>. But when there is just a little chill, a <u>shawl</u> will do.

To do:

Draw a ✂ on the ⛄.

S s

shirt

shoes

When you buy a <u>shirt</u> you usually buy one, but when you buy <u>shoes</u> you always buy two!

To do:

Draw a pair of .
Color them brown.

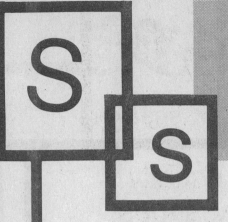

shorts

skirt

It's gym day. Sheri will wear both her <u>shorts</u> and her <u>skirt</u> today.

To do:

Color Sheri's shorts and skirt the same color.

S s

slicker

sneakers

Billy is going sailing.
He's all ready with his <u>slicker</u>
and <u>sneakers</u>.

To do: Color Billy's bright yellow.

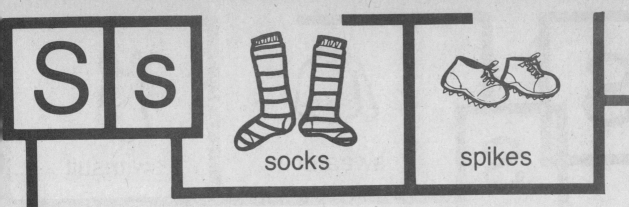

S s

socks

spikes

Sam is ready for the big game. He has his bat and ball. Now he has to find his <u>socks</u> and <u>spikes</u>!

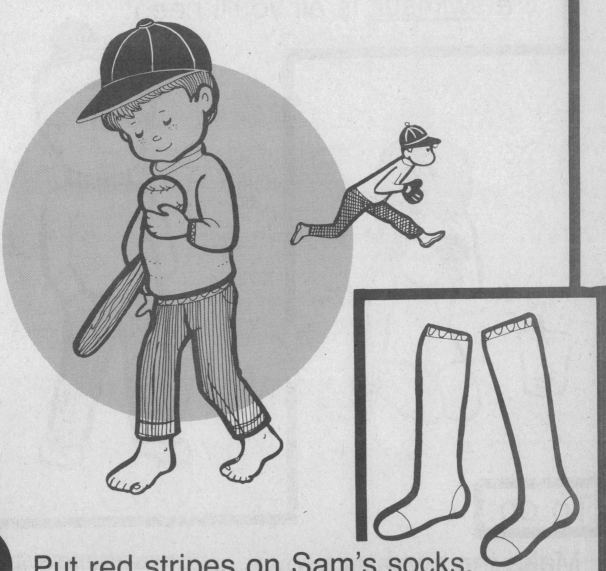

To do: Put red stripes on Sam's socks.

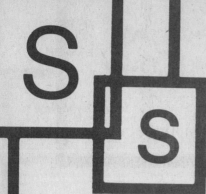

S **S**

sweater

swimsuit

If you're going to the mountains, make sure you take a <u>sweater</u>. But if you're going to the beach, a <u>swimsuit</u> is all you'll need!

To do:

Make the sweater brown and the swimsuit yellow.

tails

top hat

The President is ready for the Inauguration. He's wearing <u>tails</u> and a <u>top hat</u>. How would you like to be dressed like this?

To do:

Color the and  black.

T t

trousers

tuxedo

Dad is dressed up for a very special party. His suit has a black coat and <u>trousers</u>. It's called a <u>tuxedo</u>. Doesn't he look handsome?

To do: Draw a flower on Dad's lapel.

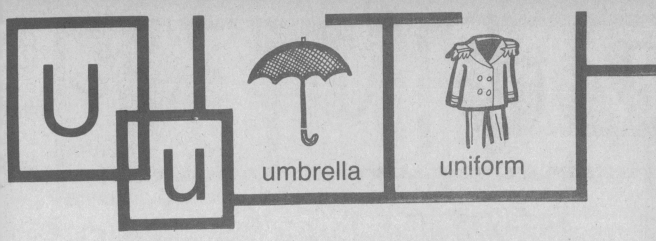

U u

umbrella

uniform

An <u>umbrella</u> is sometimes a very important part of a doorman's <u>uniform</u>.

To do:

Draw big brass  on the doorman's uniform.

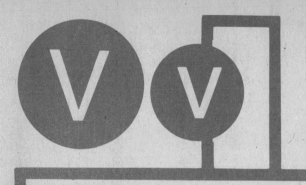 

vest   v-neck sweater

Today is the first day of school for Victor. He can't make up his mind. Should he wear his green <u>vest</u> or his brown <u>v-neck sweater</u>?

To do:

Draw a picture of what you would like to see Victor wear.

W w

waistcoat

wedding gown

Here come the bride and the groom. She looks beautiful in her <u>wedding gown</u> and he looks handsome in his <u>waistcoat</u>.

To do:

Finish the bouquet of flowers for the bride.

W w

wetsuit

windbreaker

Surf's up! You can surf in November if you wear a <u>wetsuit</u> and take along your <u>windbreaker</u>.

To do: Color the ocean blue.

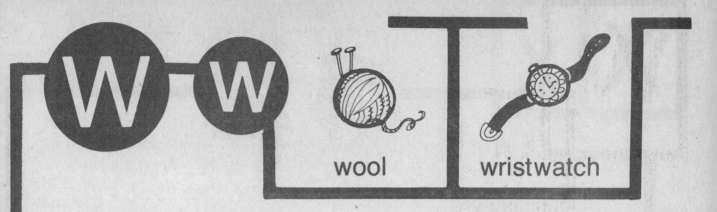

W w

wool

wristwatch

Mother and Dad are buying anniversary presents for each other. Dad will get a <u>wool</u> jacket and Mother will get a new <u>wristwatch</u>.

To do: Color Dad's wool jacket brown.

X-ray

When you have an <u>X-ray</u> taken, you may have to take off some of your clothes and put on a robe.

To do:

Draw a robe on the boy. ▶

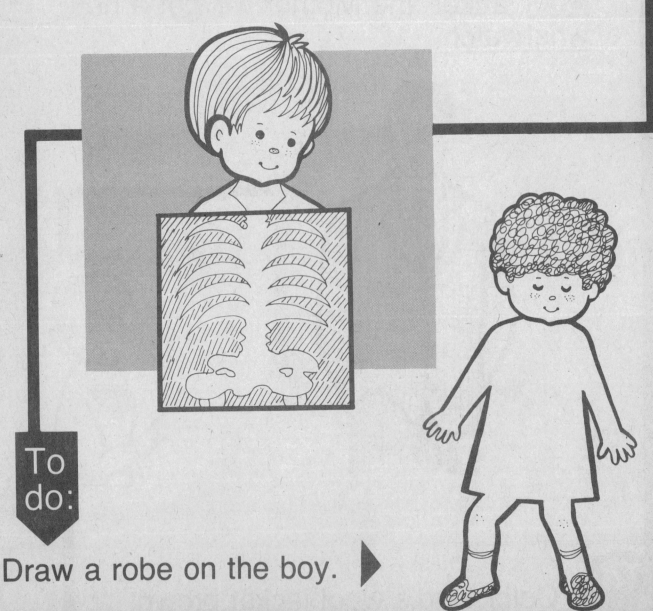

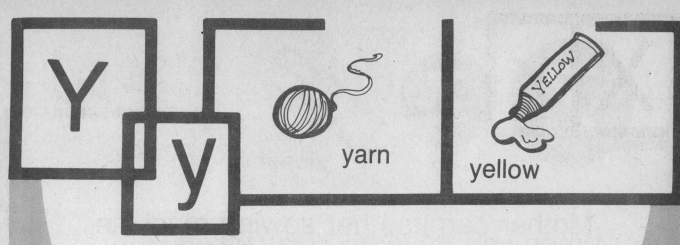

Y y

yarn

yellow

Grandma's knitting needles go "click-click" as she turns <u>yar</u>n into a beautiful <u>yellow</u> sweater.

To do: Color the yarn yellow.

Z z

zipper

zig-zag

Mother can use her sewing machine to put the <u>zipper</u> in Jennifer's new dress. She can also make a <u>zig-zag</u> stitch!

To do:

Draw a zig-zag line.

Words

Clothes We Wear

apron
ascot

belt
bermuda shorts
bib
blouse
bonnet
bootees
bow
bracelet

cap
catcher's mitt
cleats
coat
cowboy hat
crown
cuffs
cummerbund

diaper
dress

earmuffs
ears

fabric
fan
fringe
fur

galoshes
gloves
gowns
grass skirt

hard hat
helmet

ice skates
ice-skating skirt

jacket
jeans
jersey
jodhpurs

kilts
kimono
knee socks
knickers

lace
leotards

mittens
muffler

necklace
necktie
nightgown
nightshirt

opera glasses
overcoat

pajamas
pants
petticoat
pinafore

quilt
quiver

raincoat
rainhat
ribbons
rings
robe
rubbers

scarf
shawl
shirt

shoes
shorts
skirt
slicker
sneakers
socks
spikes
sweater
swimsuit

tails
top hat
trousers
tuxedo

umbrella
uniform

vest
v-neck sweater

waistcoat
wedding gown
wetsuit
windbreaker
wool
wrist watch

X-ray

yarn
yellow

zig-zag
zipper

Things That Move

THINGS THAT MOVE

Directions

When working with Things That Move, do the following:

1. Parent: On each page of the dictionary say the word or words with the corresponding picture. Have your child do the same.

2. Parent: Then read the short story to your child. Have your child find the key word or words from the page in the story.

3. Child: Complete the "To do" activity. Parent: Talk about the activity with your child.

4. Child: Color the picture and show the picture to a friend.

5. Child and Parent: Talk about the picture and the words. Ask such questions as:
   - Have you seen a _____ like that? Where?
   - Would it be a good way to travel? Why?

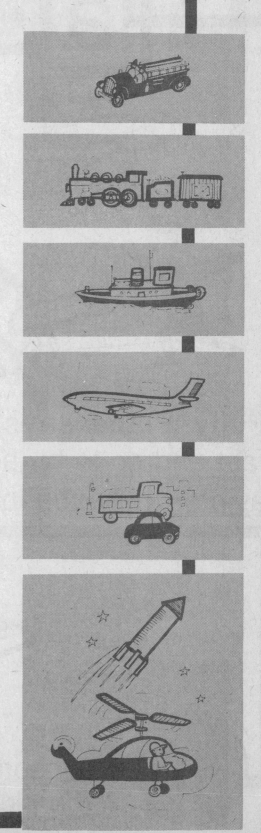

A a

airplane

aviator

Polly Plane says, "Do you want to travel fast and go to far-away places? Then ask an <u>aviator</u> to fly you in an <u>airplane</u>." Zoom!

To Do: Draw some clouds around the airplane in the picture above.

B b

barge

boat

Bobby <u>Boat</u> holds his nose when the <u>barge</u> goes by. Why? The <u>barge</u> is carrying garbage. Yuk!

To Do: Draw some birds in the picture above. They follow boats looking for free food.

B b

bus

busdriver

Billy Bus says, "Meet my friend Barney. He's a busdriver. He drives me wherever I go. And see that big bus over there? That's my pop. He's the biggest bus on the street."

To Do:
Write the word bus.

‒‒‒‒‒‒‒‒‒‒‒‒‒‒‒‒‒‒‒‒‒‒

C c

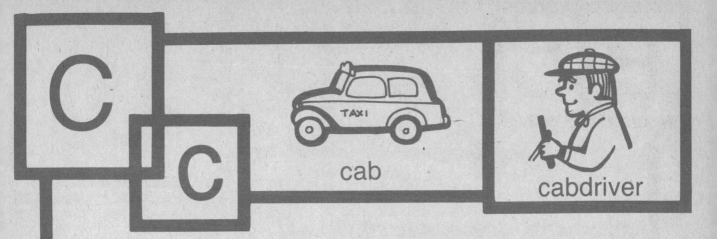

cab

cabdriver

Billy Bus says, "If you want to ride in a <u>cab</u>, have your money ready. Charlie the <u>cabdriver</u> won't let anyone have a free ride in his <u>cab</u>."

TAXI

To Do: Draw the missing wheels on the cab in the picture above.

camel

camel train

Polly Plane says, "In the desert camel trains carry people and supplies over the sand. Mmm! I think that camel is tired."

To Do: Color the camel light brown.

C c

car

Some people call me a <u>car</u>. Others call me an automobile. But I have other names too:

auto

station wagon

racing car

sports car

hot rod

To Do:

Draw a car you would like to have.

C c

coal

coal miner

Polly Plane says, "Cabs, cars and camels move and begin with C, but did you know that <u>coal</u> dug by <u>coal</u> <u>miners</u> burns and makes steam? Steam makes many things move."

To Do: Draw a pick-ax in the miner's hand in the picture above.

D d

donkey donkey cart

Polly Plane says, "In some countries the best way to travel is by <u>donkey</u> or <u>donkey</u> <u>cart</u>. One country is Brazil. Can you think of another?"

Heehaw

To Do: Color the flowers red, yellow and green.

E e

electricity

Push in the plug. Turn on the light.
Ride an electric car. Ooops! Here comes
a new train. <u>Electricity</u> makes all these
things go.

To Do: Put an X on the
thing that uses
electricity.

E e

energy

"Gasoline makes me go," says the bus.
"Wind makes me go," says the sailboat.
"Atomic __energy__ makes me go," says
the rocket. Blast off!

To Do: Color the rocket red.

E e

engine

engineer

Wo-woo-chug-a-chug! Chug-woo-woo! Billy Bus and the <u>en</u>g<u>ine</u> are having a race. The <u>en</u>g<u>ineer</u> is driving his <u>en</u>g<u>ine</u> as fast as he can.

To Do: Draw smoke coming from the engine in the picture above.

F f

ferry

Bobby Boat says, "I can carry people and things across the river, but I can't carry cars the way the big <u>ferry</u> does. Look at all the cars she can carry."

To Do: Draw another car on the ferry.

F f

fire

fire engine

Fire! Fire! Rrr-ding-ding!
Billy Bus says, "Listen to the siren.
That's a fire engine in a hurry on the
way to a fire." Rrr-ding-ding!

To Do:

Draw a fire in the picture above.

G g

gas

gasoline

Billy Bus says, "What! Out of <u>gasoline</u> again? This car won't run without <u>gas</u> and I'm getting tired of pushing it around."

GAS

To Do: Draw a hose in the picture above so that gasoline can get from the pump to the car.

G g

golf

golf cart

Polly Plane says, "Some people walk when they play <u>g</u>olf. But look at this man. He's riding in the <u>g</u>olf cart. See?"

To Do: ▶ Draw a picture of a golf club.

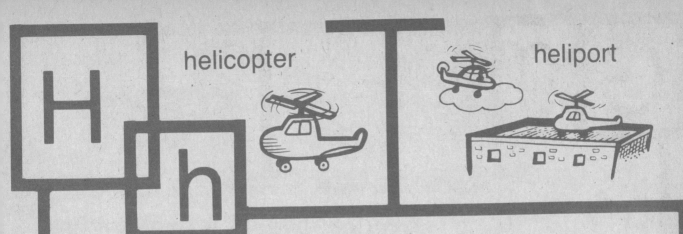

H h

helicopter

heliport

Polly Plane says, "If you want to fly and there's no airport nearby, find a <u>heliport</u> and a <u>helicopter</u> and you can fly straight up and down; even from the top of a tall building."

To Do: Draw the propeller on the helicopter in the picture above.

H h

horse

horse and buggy

Billy Bus says, "Before there were busses or cars, people traveled by <u>horse</u> <u>and</u> <u>buggy</u>. Sometimes a cowboy rode long distances on a <u>horse</u>. <u>Horses</u> couldn't go very fast, but they never ran out of gas or got flat tires."

ToDo: Draw a horse that you would like to ride.

ice cream

ice cream truck

Billy says, "Hear the bell! Here comes my favorite truck with my favorite driver. Can you name them?"

To Do: Draw pictures of your two favorite flavors of ice cream.

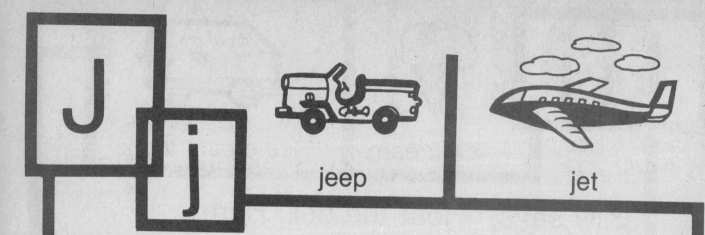

J j jeep jet

Polly Plane says, "In a race I can beat a <u>jee</u>p that travels on 4 wheels, but I don't think I can beat a <u>jet</u>, do you?"

To Do:

Add the missing parts to the picture.

K **k**

kayak

Billy Bus says, "What a strange little boat. I've never seen one like that. It looks like a banana with a hole to sit in." Bobby Boat says, "No, it's not really strange. That's a <u>kayak</u>, and they're lots of fun."

To Do:

Draw a kayak.

L l

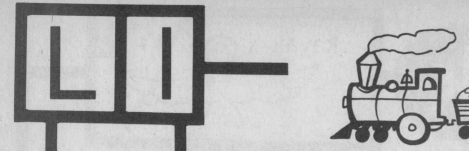

locomotive

Chug, chug, chug, chug. Polly Plane says, "Listen to the sound of the <u>locomotive</u> as it rumbles down the track." Chug, chug, chug.

To Do: The words <u>train</u> and <u>locomotive</u> mean the same thing. Write the word train.

_____

- -

_____

M m

motor

motorcycle

Rrrrrrrrr Zoom! What's all that noise? Billy Bus says, "Wow! It's a <u>motorcycle</u> with a noisy new <u>motor</u>. I wonder if it wants to race."

To Do: _____

Write the word motor. _____

_____

N n

noise

Bobby Boat says. "I have no traveling friends that begin their names with the letter N . But all my traveling friends make noise . Just listen!" "Vrrrrooooom!" says the motorcycle. "Honk, honk," says the bus. "Zoom!" goes the rocket. "Toot-toot!" says the train. "Hey, not all at once," says Bobby. "That's too much noise !"

To Do:

Draw something else that might begin with the letter n.

O o

ocean

ocean liner

Bobby Boat wants you to meet his cousin the <u>ocean liner</u>. "She's a big ship," Bobby says. "She's so big that she doesn't even rock very much when the <u>ocean</u> gets rough."

ToDo: Draw a big fish under the ocean liner in the picture above.

patrol car

police officer

The friendly <u>police</u> <u>officer</u> is waving from the <u>patrol car</u>. Billy Bus says, "He's there to help and protect us."

To Do: Write the word PO-LICE on the side of the patrol car in the picture above.

P p

pony

Pony Express

Polly Plane says, "These are <u>Pony Ex-press</u> riders. They were the first to carry the mail across the country, and they did it riding <u>ponies</u>. Do you think they have a letter for you?"

To Do:

Draw a letter <u>P</u> in the rider's hand in the picture above.

P

Q q

quiet

quietly

Polly Plane says, "I have no traveling friends that begin their names with the letter Q. But many of my traveling friends are quiet when they move. Listen. The sailboat glides quietly over the water. The camel walks quietly across the desert. A new electric train is so quiet inside that you can go to sleep."

To Do: Write the letter Q. _____

R r

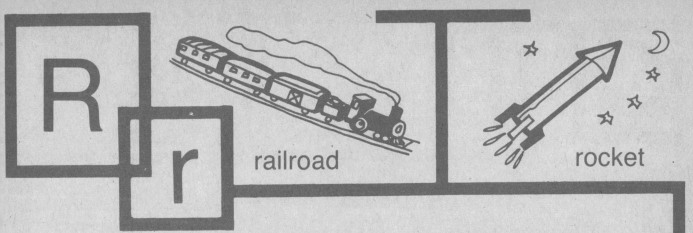

railroad

rocket

Bobby Boat says, "Many years ago the fastest way to travel was by <u>railroad</u>. But today, if you want to go really fast and really far, blast off and take a <u>rocket</u> to the moon!"

To Do:

Draw a picture of a rocket.

S s

sailboat

submarine

"Blow, wind, blow," says the <u>sailboat</u>. "Make me go as fast as you can." "Wind or storm doesn't bother me," says the <u>submarine</u>. "I travel under the water where it's calm."

To Do: Draw a big smile on Bobby Boat's face in the picture above.

T t

taxi

Billy Bus says, "I have lots of seats and I can carry many people. But sometimes people want to go where I don't go. When this happens, they take a <u>taxi</u>."

To Do: Write the word TAXI on the car in the picture above.

TAXI

T t

tractor

train

Polly Plane says, "From high in the air I watch many of my friends working hard. But no one works harder than the tractor and the train. Both the tractor and the train can pull very heavy loads. Watch them!"

To Do:

Add the missing wheels to the tractor and the train in the picture above.

T t

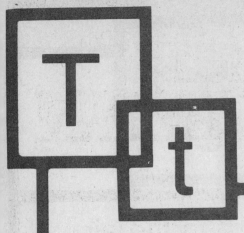

truck

tricycle

Bobby Boat asks some questions.
"Which of these is the biggest?
Which is the lightest?
Which can carry the heaviest load?
Which is the most fun to ride?
Which one carries ice cream?"

To Do: Color the truck blue.
Color the tricycle red.

U u

unicycle

"Did you lose a wheel?" asks Billy Bus. "Oh no, this is a <u>unicycle</u> and it only has one small wheel. See!"

To Do:
Make a unicycle a bicycle by adding a second wheel and handle bars. ➤

van

Billy Bus says, "Time to move? Well, call the moving <u>van</u>. Inside you can pack everything you own. Oh, no. That's much too big!"

To Do: Write the word van on the truck in the picture above.

VAN

W W

wagon

wheel

Wheels help make things move. Wheels are on wagons, buses, cars and trains. Even Polly Plane has wheels, too. Without wheels, very few things could move on land.

To Do: Color the wheels brown.

W w

wind

Bobby Boat says, "Blow, <u>wind</u>, blow! Blow fast and you will help many things move."

To Do: Write the letter W.

_____

- - - - - - - - - - - - - - -

_____

X x

Polly Plane says, "I don't have any traveling friends who begin their names with the letter <u>X</u>. Maybe someday someone will invent something that moves and begins with <u>X</u>. But until then I've drawn a picture of something I would like to ride in. I just call it <u>X</u>. Would you like to ride with me?"

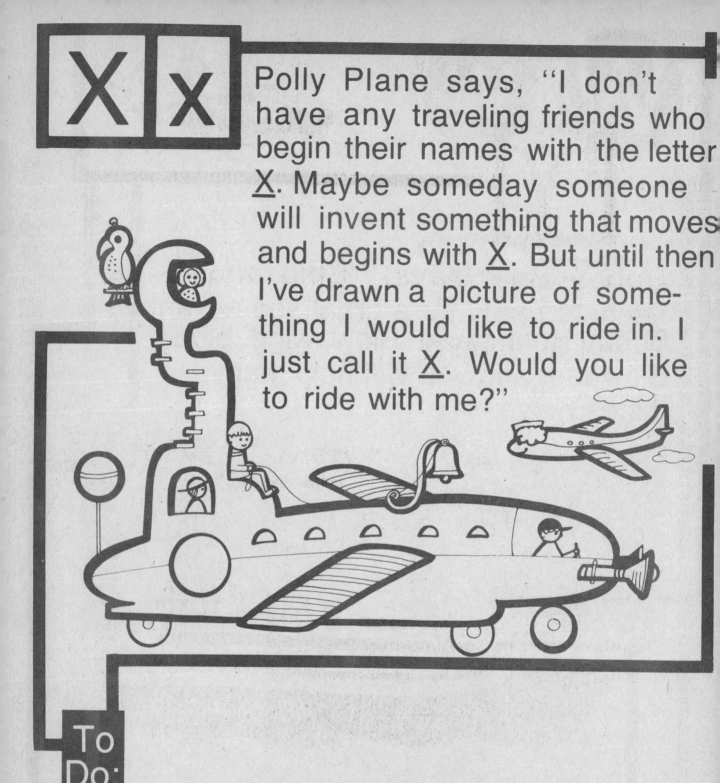

To Do:

Draw something that might begin with <u>X</u>.

Y y

yacht

Bobby Boat says, "Ship ahoy! The yacht is ready for a great sea adventure. Hurry! All aboard!"

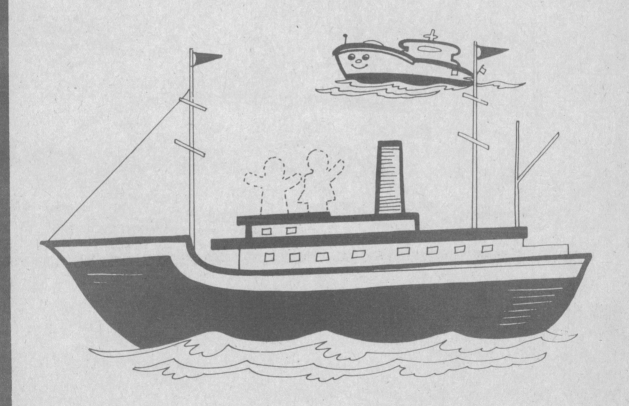

To Do: Draw more people on the yacht in the picture above.

Z z

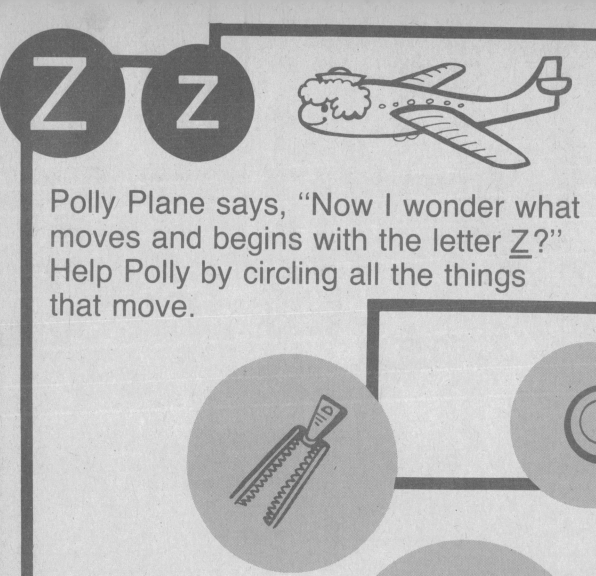

Polly Plane says, "Now I wonder what moves and begins with the letter <u>Z</u>?" Help Polly by circling all the things that move.

"Mmm, they move. But they are different from all my other traveling friends. Can you tell me how?"